AN ONI PRESS PUBLICATION
[adult swim]

POCKET LIKE YOU STOLE IT

***RICK AND MORTY*™ CREATED BY**
DAN HARMON & JUSTIN ROILAND

WRITTEN BY TINI HOWARD
ILLUSTRATED BY MARC ELLERBY
COLORED BY KATY FARINA
LETTERED BY CRANK!

RETAIL COVER BY MARC ELLERBY & KATY FARINA
ONI PRESS EXCLUSIVE COVER BY JULIETA COLÁS
FRIED PIE EXCLUSIVE COVER BY JOSCELINE FENTON

[adult swim]™

DESIGNED BY HILARY THOMPSON
EDITED BY ARI YARWOOD

PUBLISHED BY ONI PRESS, INC.
JOE NOZEMACK, FOUNDER & CHIEF FINANCIAL OFFICER
JAMES LUCAS JONES, PUBLISHER
CHARLIE CHU, V.P. OF CREATIVE & BUSINESS DEVELOPMENT
BRAD ROOKS, DIRECTOR OF OPERATIONS
RACHEL REED, MARKETING MANAGER
MELISSA MESZAROS, PUBLICITY MANAGER
TROY LOOK, DIRECTOR OF DESIGN & PRODUCTION
HILARY THOMPSON, GRAPHIC DESIGNER
KATE Z. STONE, JUNIOR GRAPHIC DESIGNER
ANGIE KNOWLES, DIGITAL PREPRESS LEAD
ARI YARWOOD, EXECUTIVE EDITOR
ROBIN HERRERA, SENIOR EDITOR
DESIREE WILSON, ASSOCIATE EDITOR
ALISSA SALLAH, ADMINISTRATIVE ASSISTANT
JUNG LEE, LOGISTICS ASSOCIATE

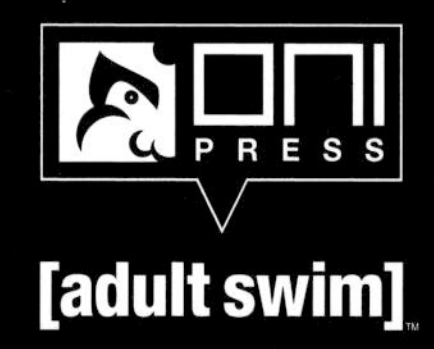

[adult swim]™

ONIPRESS.COM
FACEBOOK.COM/ONIPRESS
TWITTER.COM/ONIPRESS
ONIPRESS.TUMBLR.COM
INSTAGRAM.COM/ONIPRESS

THIS VOLUME COLLECTS ISSUES #1–5 OF THE ONI PRESS SERIES
RICK AND MORTY™: POCKET LIKE YOU STOLE IT.

FIRST EDITION: MARCH 2018

ISBN 978-1-62010-474-3
EISBN 978-1-62010-475-0
ONI PRESS EXCLUSIVE ISBN 978-1-62010-491-0
FRIED PIE EXCLUSIVE ISBN 978-1-62010-498-9

PRINTED IN CHINA.

LIBRARY OF CONGRESS CONTROL NUMBER: 2017949065

1 2 3 4 5 6 7 8 9 10

SPECIAL THANKS TO JUSTIN ROILAND, DAN HARMON, MARISA MARIONAKIS, MIKE MENDEL, AND JANET NO.

CHAPTER ONE

THE AGONY OF FREEDOM

DAY 14

NO, MORTYYYY, DON'T LEEEEAVE ME.
IT'S SO DARK, I DON'T WANNA BE ALONE!

YOU NEED FOOD, MER-MORTY! AND-AND-AND WATER?

SINCE I'M PRETTY SURE YOU'RE PART FISH?

LISTEN! LISTEN TO ME. I-I-I'LL BE RIGHT BACK, OKAY.
WITH-WITH WATER! A-A-AND FOOD! AND MEDICINE! AND UH, LIKE, A CROSSWORD PUZZLE OR SOMETHING, YOU GOTTA BE BORED.

I'M GOIN' CRAZY DOWN HERE.

ACTUALLY, I THINK CROSSWORD PUZZLES ONLY EXIST ON AIRPLANES, ANYMORE.
JUICE
OHHH MAN.
I GOT THIS, MER-MORTY.
JUICE
CHUMBOS
Pretz

Pretz
CHUMBOS
JUICE
FOR YOU. FOR ME. FOR--
WHAP

RICK A MORTY
& THE PO MORTYS IN:
POCKET LIKE YOU STOLE IT!
PART ONE: HORRIBLE FREEDOM
SCRIPT: TINI HOWARD
ART: MARC ELLERBY
COLORS: KATY FARINA
LETTERS: CRANK!
WUBBA LUBBA DUB DUB!!
ZZZRRT

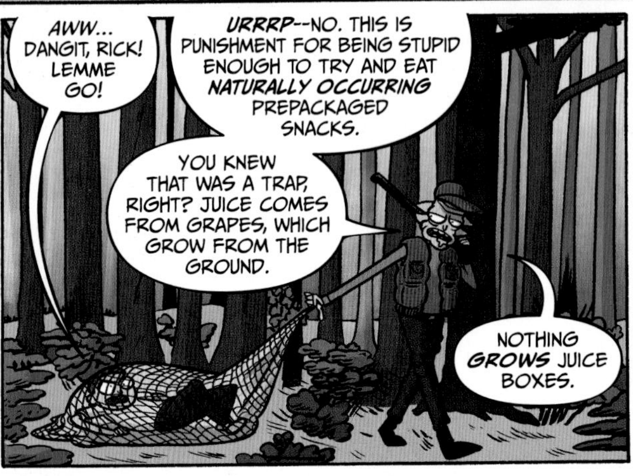
AWW... DANGIT, RICK! LEMME GO!
URRRP--NO. THIS IS PUNISHMENT FOR BEING STUPID ENOUGH TO TRY AND EAT NATURALLY OCCURRING PREPACKAGED SNACKS.
YOU KNEW THAT WAS A TRAP, RIGHT? JUICE COMES FROM GRAPES, WHICH GROW FROM THE GROUND.
NOTHING GROWS JUICE BOXES.

JUICE IS JUST AN IDIOT STOPPING POINT BETWEEN FRUIT AND ALCOHOL.
RICK!

YOU GOTTA LET ME GO! IT WASN'T FOR ME!
THE SNACKS WERE FOR--

WHO'S IT FOR, MORTY?
GO ON AND TELL ME. YOU GOT A LITTLE FRIEND OUT THERE FOR ME TO CATCH, MORTY?

AH-N-NO! NO, NOPE, NUH-UH.
J-J-JUST ME, RICK. HEH.

THAT'S WHAT I *THOUGHT.*

I'M SO, SO SORRY, MER-MORTY. IT'S BETTER THIS WAY...

...*WHEREVER* YOU ARE...

BAM

SAY HI, MORTYS.

HIIIIII, MORTYYYS.

DANGIT RICK! THIS ISN'T SUPER BANANA FARM!
SUPER-- SUPER WHAT?

IT'S... IT'S A PHONE GAME...
IZZAT SOME KINDA... KINDA META-COMMENTARY ON THE SITUATION IN WHICH WE CURRENTLY FIND OURSELVES?

RICK, I'M A TERRIBLE FIGHTER! I'VE NEVER WON A MORTY BATTLE, SO JUST LET ME GO!
MORTY, YOU REALIZE THERE'S AN ENTIRE UNIVERSE WHERE EVERYONE--MAN, WOMAN, CHILD--WALK ON THEIR HANDS AND RIP EACH OTHER'S THROATS OUT WITH THEIR TEETH WHEN THEY GET HUNGRY?

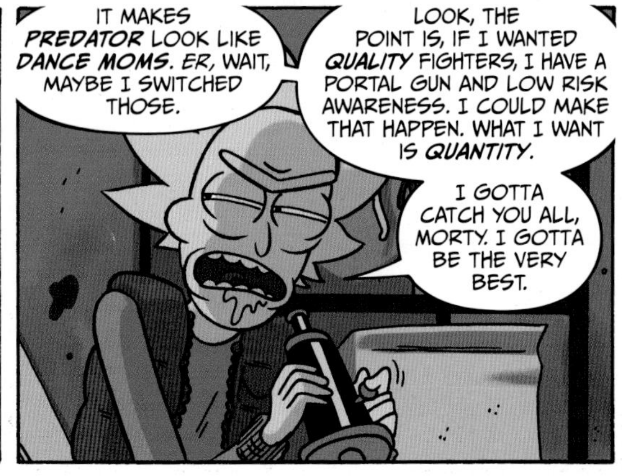
IT MAKES PREDATOR LOOK LIKE DANCE MOMS. ER, WAIT, MAYBE I SWITCHED THOSE.
LOOK, THE POINT IS, IF I WANTED QUALITY FIGHTERS, I HAVE A PORTAL GUN AND LOW RISK AWARENESS. I COULD MAKE THAT HAPPEN. WHAT I WANT IS QUANTITY.
I GOTTA CATCH YOU ALL, MORTY. I GOTTA BE THE VERY BEST.

AND, UH, THERE ARE SOME PEOPLE I WANT DEAD.

WHAT ABOUT SUMMER? ISN'T SHE SOME SORT OF INTERDIMENSIONAL BADASS?

I TRIED THAT, MORTY. BELIEVE ME.
WHRRREEEEEE

LET'S JUST SAY IT'S A GOOD THING I WEAR A CUP. AND GROW EXTRA ORGANS IN THE LAB, FOR JUST SUCH AN OCCASION. ACTUALLY, MORTY, DO YOU STILL HAVE YOUR--

OH, BALLS.

PANT
PANT
PANT

ZZZRT
AAHHH... NO!

I DON'T WANNA!
HEY--IT'S LOOSE!

HEYYYY... RICK MUST'VE BEEN WASTED WHEN HE LOADED THE GUN! THE-THE THING! THAT'S WHY IT'S NOT CONTROLLING MY THOUGHTS!

HNNNGH!
MORTY, DON'T MAKE ME CHA--URRRP--ASE YOU!

EVEN-- EVEN I HAVE PRIDE!

SKIIIIIIIIIID

SLAM

PANT
PANT
PANT

H-H-HEY THERE!!
AAAAUGH!

S-SORRY. I ASSUME YOU AREN'T A RICK BECAUSE YOU DON'T SMELL LIKE GIN.
I CAN'T TELL, THOUGH. I CAN'T SEE A DARN THING.
C-CLICK

ON ACCOUNT OF ALL THE *ANTS IN MY EYES.*

RIGHT, *UH,* WHY ARE YOU HIDING IN HERE?

UH, WELL, I'M TRYING TO ESCAPE, BUT I CAN'T SEE VERY WELL.
ON ACCOUNT OF ALL THE--

YEAH, I GOT IT. *HEY,* WAIT.
HOW COME YOU AREN'T ZAPPED BY THE CHIP FOR RUNNING OFF?

ONE OF THESE.
OH, I-- I MIGHT BE. I DUNNO. I CAN'T FEEL A THING. IT'S RELATED TO THE ANTS IN MY EYES, BUT NOT AS--NOT AS CATCHY.

LISTEN TO ME, ANTS IN MY EYES MORTY. WE'RE GONNA GET OUT OF HERE, OKAY? YOU AND ME.
SURE, THAT SOUNDS GREAT. I THINK. EVERYTHING'S BLACK.

AW, GEEZ. C'MON.

SORRY, MORTY, I COULDN'T SEE YA.
ON ACCOUNT OF--

?!

OH MAN.
HUH? IS THAT YOU?

YEAH, ANTS IN MY EYES MORTY. WE'RE FINE.
RICK ONLY COMES DOWN THIS WAY TO TAKE A POOP.

WHICH MEANS WE'VE GOT TIL SPLASHDOWN TO FREE THE OTHERS.

LET'S GO!
YOU'RE GONNA HAVE TO LEAD THE WAY, THOUGH. ON--
I KNOW.

C'MON!

OH GOD. IT'S ALREADY SO HARD TO COME BACK TO THIS PLACE.
WHERE? ARE WE IN THE COMMODE?
IT SMELLS LIKE THE COMMODE.

NO, ANTS IN MY EYES MORTY! HERE!
THE PLACE WHERE OUR FREEDOM WAS KEPT FROM US!
Z

OIL...
CAN...

SH-SHOULD I LEAVE THIS HERE?
A HORRIFYING CROSS BETWEEN A ZOO AND AN OUBLIETTE OF HORRORS!

A... A ZOOBLIETTE!

ZOOBLIETTE? WORDS LIKE THAT ARE FOR AGES TEN AND UP, MORTY.
RICK!
I'M ACTUALLY LIKE, UH, FOURTEEN, I THINK?
I LITERALLY DON'T CARE.
FIND A CAGE, MORTY. ANTS IN MY EYES MORTY.
CHK CHK

OH, OKAY. THIS A CAGE? I CAN'T REALLY SEE.

THIS IS EVIL, RICK. YOU'RE SICK.

NO MORE SO THAN ONE OF THE MOST BELOVED VIDEO GAME FRANCHISES OF THE LAST TWENTY YEARS, *MORTY.*

I CAN'T HANDLE THIS ANYMORE, RICK! I'M NEVER GONNA FIGHT FOR YOU, STUPID CHIP OR NOT!

FINE.
GO ON. RUN AWAY.
RICK...?

I DON'T UNDERSTAND.
YOU WANNA GO, GO.

I CAN'T!
I CAN'T JUST *LEAVE* ALL OF THESE MORTYS!

GO AHEAD. TAKE 'EM WITH YOU.
SUPPLIES

MY, *UH*... BROTHERS? OR WHATEVER YOU ARE!
MORTYS! YOU DESERVE, *UH*, OTHER STUFF!
NOT THIS!
WHUMP

COME WITH ME! LET US REMOVE YOUR MANIPULATION CHIPS! WITHOUT THEM, WE'RE *FREE!*

SEE?!
!!
YANK

NO! NO NO NO NO, OH GOD, ANTS IN MY EYES MORTY, SAY SOMETHING!
GASP!
N-N-NO!
PLEASE, GOD, DON'T LET EVIL MORTY HURT ME!

N-N-NO! I'M NOT EVIL MORTY!
THAT GUY'S EVIL MORTY!

HMM... PERHAPS.

URRRP--AH-YEP, MORTY. THERE YOU GO AGAIN.
DOIN' MY JOB FOR ME WITH YOUR OWN STUPIDITY.

NO. I'M A BAD FIGHTER, RICK, YOU'RE RIGHT.

BUT I HAVE TO FIND SOMETHING I'M GOOD AT. I CAN'T JUST BE... PLAIN MORTY.
AND I'M NOT EVIL MORTY.

"I REFUSE TO FIGHT. ALL I NEED IS SOMEWHERE I CAN JUST BE."

I'M... I'M FREE?

I'LL FIND **SOMEWHERE** I CAN GO.

SOMEWHERE WHE-WHERE I CAN JUST BE **MORTY**, YOU KNOW? AND REALLY...

...FIND MYSELF?
NEXT: THE MARVELOUS WORLD OF MORTY COLLECTOR!

CHAPTER TWO

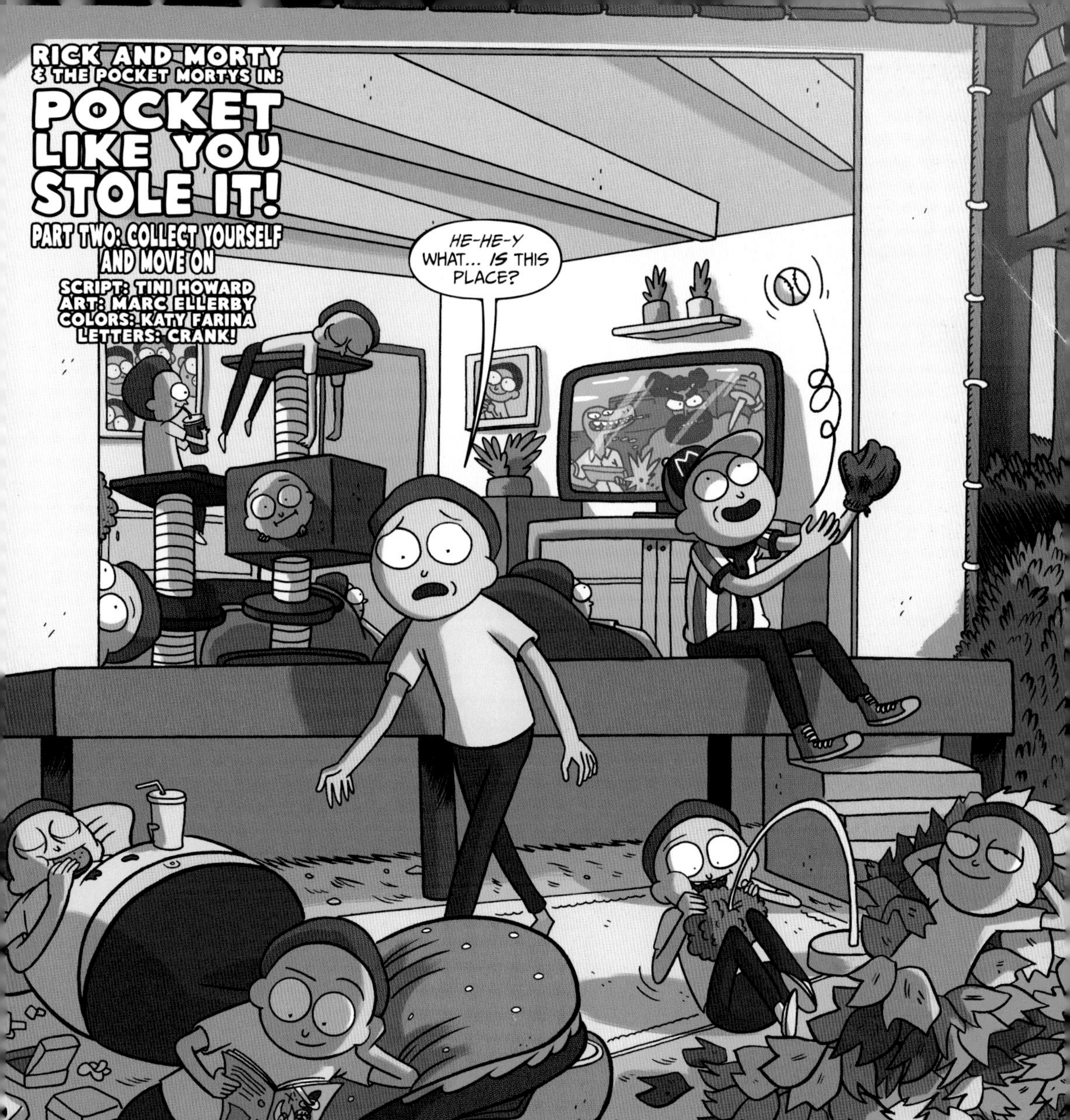
RICK AND MORTY
& THE POCKET MORTYS IN:
POCKET LIKE YOU STOLE IT!
PART TWO: COLLECT YOURSELF AND MOVE ON
SCRIPT: TINI HOWARD
ART: MARC ELLERBY
COLORS: KATY FARINA
LETTERS: CRANK!
HE-HE-Y WHAT... *IS* THIS PLACE?

THEY'RE ALL JUST... EATING SNACKS...

...IN DUMB LITTLE HATS?!

AWW, GEEZ... WHAT A SOOTHING WASTE OF TIME.
JUST WHAT I NEED!

HE-HE-HEY THERE, FRIEND! HEH, MIND IF I SHARE THAT SUNBEAM?

FRP

HUH? HEY, CALM DOWN, DON'T HURT YOURSELF!

N-NO! NOT AGAIN! I DON'T WANNA KILL ANOTHER ONE!
I DIDN'T DO ANYTHING!

N-NO... NOT AGAIN... NO NO!
WHOA, SHHH.

THERE'S NO CRYING IN MORTY COLLECTOR.
WH-WHAT'S MORTY COLLECTOR?

THIS IS MORTY COLLECTOR.

PUT THIS ON BEFORE WE GET IN TROUBLE.

TR-TROUBLE?

YEAH. TROUBLE.
OH *MAN*... I'M TRYING TO GET *OUT* OF SOME KINDA TROUBLE, FRIEND--

SHH. HE'S COMING.
MHOO?

DADDY'S HOME!
HEY, WOW, GEEZ! IT'S CRAZY CAT RICK!

HOW ARE MY CHUBBY LITTLE CASTOFFS TODAY?
I SWEAR, LOOK AT YOU. IF THERE WERE A GOD, AND THAT GOD HAD AN EMBARRASSING NOTEBOOK OF *MAGIC: THE GATHERING* FANFICTION, AND THAT NOTEBOOK BECAME A FULLY REALIZED PERSON, IT WOULD BE EACH AND EVERY ONE OF YOU.
THAAAAANK YOU, RIIIIIICK.

NOW. WHO HAS SOMETHING FOR DADDY TODAY?

HUH? ARE WE SUPPOSED TO GIVE HIM STUFF? CAN I CLAIM REFUGEE STATUS?
CLOCKING OUT?
WHUH? OH, I'M JUST CLOCKING OUT.
YEAH. LEAVING. I GOT A WIFE AND KIDS BACK HOME.

G'NIGHT, CHOO CHOO MORTY! DON'T DO ANYTHING I WOULDN'T DO! *HEH*, LITTLE--*URRRP*-- TROUBLEMAKER.
WIFE AND KIDS?!

UHHHH...

UH... HEY, CRAZY CAT RICK.
SQUISH
SQUISH

YOU'RE NEW HERE.
I... UH. YEAH. HEH. YOU GOT ME.

ALL RIGHT!
A NEW MORTY!
OH, WOW, I TRIED LAYING OUT THE CHICK PILLOW WITH THE BAZOOMS, AND THEN THE LITTLE STUPID VIDEO GAME, YOU KIDS JUST LOVE THAT PIECE OF CRAP, AND I WASN'T GETTING ANY NEW MORTYS!
BUT FINALLY, A NEW ONE!

YESSSSSS!
YEAH, YEAH. I'M A MORON, OKAY, RICK? I WAS TRICKED BY THE NICE STUFF.
JUST TELL ME WHO I HAVE TO FIGHT.

FIGHT? YOU KIDDIN' ME? HAVE YOU SEEN YOURSELF?
I'VE PUKED UP STUFF AFTER BEING PUNCHED IN THE STOMACH THAT WAS MORE DANGEROUS THAN YOU.

THAT'S WHAT *I'VE* BEEN SAYING THIS *WHOLE TIME!*
GEEZ, RICK, I NEVER THOUGHT I'D MEET ANOTHER ONE OF YOU THAT I WASN'T SCARED OF, *HEH*, BUT YOU HAVE YOUR HEAD ON STRAIGHT.

HUNH? OH, YEAH, SURE. YOU'RE FINE.
HERE, EAT SOME KIBBLE.
MORTY BITS
MORTY

WELLLL, I GUESS I AM A BIT HUNGRY. I SHOULD EAT.
MORTY

NOT A BAD PLACE YOU FIND YOURSELF, MORTY.

NOT BAD AT ALL.

LATER.

HEY, LITTLE BUDDY. YOU GET LOST LOOKING FOR A LITTERBOX?
LITTERBOX? OH, *UH*, I JUST WENT IN THE LITTLE FOAM TOILET...

THAT WAS A TOY, MORTY. FOR THE ***OTHER MORTYS***. IT DOESN'T EVEN HAVE PLUMBING.
HEH... YEAH. I NOTICED THAT... AFTER?
ANYWAY, I'VE GOT PLACES TO BE, AND--

THEN.
PAY.
UP.
HUH?!

YOU THINK ALL THESE SCRATCHING POSTS AND FOAM TOILETS AND ANIME BODY PILLOWS PAY FOR THEMSELVES? JESUS, MORTYS ARE DUMB.
THIS IS AN ECONOMY, KID. YOU COME HERE, YOU ENJOY IT, YOU PAY UP WHEN YOU LEAVE.
ABOUT THAT--

THAT DOESN'T REALLY SEEM FAIR. IT JUST LOOKED SO NICE, I DIDN'T KNOW WE HAD TO PAY FOR IT...

I FEEL LIKE THIS IS WHERE ANYONE ELSE WOULD MAKE A GENERAL--URRRRRP--IZATION ABOUT MILLENIAL ENTITLEMENT, AND I'D HAVE TO CORRECT THEM THAT THE PROBLEM IS REALLY JUST MORTYS.
DON'T WORRY. I GOT A PLAN FOR YOU.

AW, GEEZ, REALLY? I KNEW YOU WERE BETTER THAN THE OTHER RICKS, CRAZY CAT RICK.

I MEAN, IT'S EASY TO ASSUME *ALL* RICKS ARE JUST GONNA BE REAL JERKS, YOU KNOW?
BUT THERE'S A REASON WE GO TOGETHER, YOU KNOW, RICK? LIKE-LIKE-LIKE SONNY AND CHER!
OR, *UH,* SIEGFRIED AND ROY!
PANTS OFF.

SURE, SURE. ANYWAY, I REALLY APPRECIATE THIS, 'CAUSE I JUST DON'T HAVE ANY SCHMECKLES ON ME, AND I GOTTA HEAD OUT OF HERE TO SAVE THE OTHER MORTYS AND--
UNDERPANTS, TOO.

HEH, OKAAAY. I TRUST YOU, RICK, YOU KNOW I'VE GOT MORTYS TO SAVE--
DINGUS MORTIMUS

LOTTA MORTYS GET ROWDY WITH ME BEFORE THEY'VE BEEN NEUTERED.

OH NO YOU DON'T!
UN-NEUTERED EVIL MORTYS ARE THE RAREST OF ALL!
AW, GEEZ, I'M NOT EVIL MORTY!

YOU'LL FEEL MUCH BETTER WHEN I'M DONE, MORTY.
I KNOW I WILL.

BEEP BEEP BEEP

DAMMIT. ONE OF THE MORTYS FOUND A BOX HE ALMOST DOESN'T FIT IN. THAT'S SO CUTE, I GOTTA GO SEE.

I'LL BE BACK FOR YOU.

ONWARD, I GUESS.
LOTSA RICKS TO ESCAPE.

THE OTHER MORTYS TO SAVE.

MY NARDS TO PROTECT.

AW, GEEZ... ANOTHER RICK. I CAN'T TAKE THE CHANCE.

YOU HAVE NOTH--URRRP--ING TO FEAR, LITTLE MORTIMER. C'MON AND GET OVER HERE.

UHHHHMMM...
NAH, IT'S LIKE THIS: OHMMMM.

DAMMIT. ANOTHER RICK.
WHY DOES THIS KEEP HAPPENING TO ME?

BETTER QUESTION: WHY DO YOU KEEP HAPPENING UPON RICKS?

HUH?
YOU'RE TRYING TO SAVE MORTYS, AND YOU KEEP ENCOUNTERING RICKS.
EVER THINK OF *WH--URRRP--* *WHY?*

AW, GEEZ, HIPPIE RICK, IT SMELLS LIKE CAT PEE UP HERE. I GOT ENOUGH OF THAT SMELL WITH MY LAST RICK.
IT'S *KOMBUCHA,* MORTY.
IT'S SUPER GOOD FOR YOU.
AND IF YOU DRINK ENOUGH OF IT YOU CATCH A BU-- *URRRRRP--* UZZ.

OKAY, SO. ENOUGH OF THE DEEP THOUGHTS. JUST TELL ME WHO I HAVE TO FIGHT, OR WHERE MY BALLS HAVE TO GO, OR WHATEVER.
I'M TIRED OF THIS, HIPPIE RICK. I'M TIRED OF *RICKS.*

FIGHT? *NAH, MORTY,* I DON'T FIGHT. I'M OVER IT.
ME AND MY MORTYS LIVE COMMUNALLY HERE. THEY FARM THE KOMBUCHA I NEED TO STAY NICE AND BUZZED, AND I DON'T MAKE 'EM FIGHT.
SO, SLAVE LABOR?
NAAHHHHH.
JUST... *NAH?*
NAAHHHHH.

KOMBUCHA? DRINK UP, IT'S STORYTIME.
CHECK IT OUT, THE MORTYS PUT LITTLE MOTIVATIONAL MESSAGES UNDER THE CAP.

WOW, *HUH*.
THIS IS PRETTY OKAY I GUESS

ANYWAY, OUR STORY STARTS LONG AGO, BACK WHEN THIS PLACE WAS *PRETTY* DIFFERENT...

A LONG TIME AGO, BUT LIKE, STILL RIGHT HERE.
DO YOU NOTICE ANYTHING *STRANGE?*
UH, NO, HIPPIE RICK, I CAN'T SEE INTO YOUR VISION. YOU'RE JUST TELLING A STORY, REMEMBER?
OH, RIGHT. THERE AREN'T ANY RICKS OR MORTYS.
OH. *UH*, OKAY?

GEEZ, MORTY, WE'VE MANAGED TO GET THROUGH THIS WHOLE THING WITH ALMOST *NO* EXPOSITION, YOU WANNA LET ME HAVE THIS?
ALL RIGHT, GEEZ, SORRY.

SO, THIS REALITY HAS ALWAYS BEEN BASED ON THE IDEA OF TRAINERS AND PETS. EVERYONE HERE GREW UP TRAINING AND BATTLING THE CUTE LITTLE WILDLIFE THAT OCCURS NATURALLY, AND IT BECOMES THE DRIVING FORCE BEHIND THE ECONOMY. PEOPLE MAKE GYMS, COMFORTABLE TRAINING GEAR, AND RESTRAINTS THAT YOUR LITTLE MONSTERS CAN'T CHEW THROUGH.

BUT OVER TIME, THE TRAINERS DISCOVERED THAT THERE WAS *ONE* TYPE OF LITTLE PET THAT WAS FIERCER THAN ALL THE OTHERS. SMARTER, MORE VIOLENT, MORE DANGEROUS. THERE WAS NO POINT IN EVEN *TRAINING* A MONSTER, UNLESS...

UNLESS YOU HAD ONE OF THESE...
ONE OF WHAT?
I CAN'T... I CAN'T SEE THE--

JESUS, MORTY, IT'S A RICK. IT'S A POCKET RICK, THAT'S THE WHOLE DAMN POINT OF THE STORY, THAT THERE USED TO BE POCKET RICKS.

I SHOULDA--URRRP-- SHOULDA JUST SAID THAT, NO APPRECIATION FOR STORYTELLING.

IT DIDN'T TAKE LONG FOR THE POCKET RICKS TO TEAR EVERY OTHER LITTLE PET APART.

YIP
YIP
AWOOO!
AAHAHH! HAAAAAHAHHAHAA. GRRRRRR.

SOON ENOUGH, ALL THE OTHER PETS WERE DEAD, AND IT WAS JUST RICK-ON-RICK ACTION.

AUUUGH! OH GOD!
WHY WOULD SOMETHING WE FOUGHT FOR SPORT EVER TURN ON US?!
IT DIDN'T TAKE LONG FOR THE RICKS TO DECIDE THEY WEREN'T FIGHTING FOR ANYONE ELSE, EVER AGAIN.

WHEN THE RICKS REBELLED, THEY MEANT IT.

BUT WHEN THE BATTLE WAS WON, THEY STILL CRAVED FIGHTING.
AND KNEW *JUST* WHERE TO GET THEIR NEW COMBATANTS.
MORTY

SLURRRRRP

URRRRRP.
WELL?!
WHAT?

SO WHAT YOU'RE SAYING IS I NEED TO GATHER THE OTHER MORTYS AND REBEL, RIGHT?
OH, NO.

ME, I HATE VIOLENCE. BESIDES... THE RICKS FIGURED THIS MIGHT HAPPEN AGAIN, SO. THEY PUT IN A FAILSAFE.
FAILSAFE? WHAT KIND OF FAILSAFE?

A FAILSAFE MADE OF *TOTAL DICKS*.
NEXT: SHADOWY COUNCILS ARE ALWAYS BAD

POCKET LIKE YOU STOLE IT

CHAPTER THREE

RICK AND MORTY & THE POCKET MORTYS IN:

POCKET LIKE YOU STOLE IT!

PART THREE: CRISIS ON INFINITE DADS!

SCRIPT: TINI HOWARD
ART: MARC ELLERBY
COLORS: KATY FARINA
LETTERS: CRANK!

NOW, WHERE WERE WE?
RIGHT. COUNCIL OF RICKS.
SIX MOP-TOP LADS WITH A TASTE FOR SUPER SCIENCE AND AVOIDING PERSONAL RESPONSIBILITY.

AND A LUST FOR VIOLENCE! OR, AT LEAST...
...A REAL NEED FOR ENTERTAINMENT, AND A SORT OF MODERN NUMBNESS TOWARD VIOLENCE.
WAIT, THERE'S A *SYSTEM?*
THEY'RE NOT JUST BATTLING US TO BE... *RICKS* ABOUT IT?
PARAMORTY!

WHAT DO YOU MEAN? EVEN IN A BEST CASE SCENARIO, YOU'RE JUST A GUINEA PIG BUT WITH THE ADDED FUN OF PUBERTY.
I MEAN THAT THEY'RE ALL BATTLING US MORTYS FOR A *REASON!* THEY'RE *GUIDED* TO IT BY THIS COUNCIL!
EVEN YOU'RE HERE IN HIDING SO YOU DON'T *HAVE TO!*

SO?
SO?! SO IF THERE'S NO COUNCIL, YOU ALL WILL JUST DO WHATEVER! DRINK, OR, OR-OR BUILD BABY TAZERS, FOR BABIES!
I GOTTA TAKE DOWN THAT COUNCIL, HIPPIE RICK. THE RICKS DON'T HAVE THE ATTENTION SPAN TO KEEP DOWN A BUNCH OF MORTYS ON THEIR OWN.

YOU'RE ALL JUST SLAVES! SLAVES TO THE *RICK SYSTEM!* I'LL FREE MORTYS AND RICKS BOTH!

YEAH? AT LEAST WE DON'T HAVE TO WEAR SHOCK CHIPS AND LIVE IN LITTLE CAT CARRIERS, MORTY.

YOU WANNA, YOU WANNA INSINU--*URRRP*--ATE THAT YOU'VE GOT IT TOGETHER MORE THAN WE DO, MORTY?
EVEN OUTSIDE OF THIS REALITY, I HEAR THAT MORTYS PRETTY MUCH CAN'T BE TRUSTED ALONE WITH AN UNDERWEAR CATALOG.

H-HEY, THE SCHOOL COUNSELOR SAID SHE WOULDN'T TELL ANYONE ABOUT THAT...

ALL THINGS ARE KNOWN TO THE AKASHIC RECORD, MORTIMER.

SOOO... I'M GONNA GO FIGHT THAT COUNCIL, NOW.
SURE, WHATEVER, I JUST FARM HERE, KID.

AW, GEEZ.

HERE'S A MAP.
GYM
HIPPIE MOUNTAIN
MORTY COLLECTOR
STRIP BAR 7/10
BAR
STRIP BAR 6/10
BURRITOS
STAN'S
BAR
"SECRET" LAB
BAR
STRIP BAR 10/10
GYM
GYM
COUNCIL OF RICKS
PIZZAS
STRIP BAR 8.2/10
W
S
SO THERE'S THE COUNCIL.
I CAN'T GATHER THE OTHER MORTYS TO REBEL ALONG WITH ME.
PUTTING ANOTHER MORTY IN HARM'S WAY WOULD MAKE ME NO BETTER THAN A RICK.
UHH...
I WAS JUST TRYING TO SHOW YOU HOW TO GET OFF THE MOUNTAIN SO YOU COULD LEAVE.
I'M KIND OF TIRED OF WEARING PANTS NOW.
I'LL HAVE TO DESTROY THE COUNCIL ALL BY MYSELF.
NO, I DIDN'T--
I'LL DO IT.
AH, YEP.
PANTS... OFF.

I WAS FOOLISH TO EVER THINK I COULD ORGANIZE THE OTHER MORTYS.
MY PEOPLE NEED A-A-A **HERO**, ONE ALONE WHO CAN TAKE ON THE COUNCIL OF RICKS.

AND THEN THE RICKS CAN GO BACK TO JUST... BEING **REGULAR** OL' DOUCHEBAGS. UNORGANIZED. AND STUFF.
SERIOUSLY?

I KNOW THAT VOICE.
DON'T TELL ME YOU FORGOT **ALREADY**.

WE'VE BEEN **OVER** THIS, YOU SLEEP IN THE **DOG BED**.

NOT.
IN.
MY.
LAUNDRY.
WHIIIINE

MOMMY?!

OH, CRAP.

HI, MORTY.

MORTY. I REALLY HOPED YOU WOULDN'T SEE YOUR FATHER AND I LIKE THIS.
I'M SOHAPPY TOSEEYOU I'MONTHERUN ANDI'MTRYING TOTAKEDOWN ANEVILEMPIRE OFGRANDPA RICKS!

OH. BECAUSE IT'S... WEIRD, AND KIND OF REFLECTIVE OF OTHER PARTS OF YOUR RELATIONSHIP DYNAMIC?
WELL, SURE. AND ALSO...
...JERRY BATTLING ISN'T SANCTIONED IN THIS REALITY SO WE HAVE TO TRAIN IN SECRET.

AW, GROSS, SICK!
MOM!

WHAT? WHAT, MORTY? WHAT'S SO BAD ABOUT THIS?
WHY DO YOU HAVE SO MANY, WHERE DID YOU EVEN GET ALL OF THESE JERRYS?

POCKET JERRYS. AND IT'S FUNNY YOU SHOULD ASK...

YOU KNOW THERE ARE JUST ENTIRE *FACILITIES* OF THESE GUYS *ALL OVER REALITY?*

A WHOLE DAYCARE FULL OF JERRYS! PEOPLE JUST *LEFT* THEM THERE.
YOU WALK IN AND SAY YOU'RE THERE TO TAKE THEM HOME AND THEY ALL JUST WANT TO COME WITH YOU.

UHH...
NOT LIKE I'D *KNOW,* BUT...
DON'T... *UH...* I MEAN, *WOULDN'T* THOSE PLACES HAVE SOME SORT OF *SYSTEM,* TO *PREVENT* PEOPLE TAKING JERRYS THAT DON'T BELONG TO THEM?
I *DON'T KNOW,* MORTY.

DO THEY??
HEH! NO IDEA! JUST... JUST A THOUGHT... NO... I WOULDN'T... WOULDN'T KNOW...

THAT'S WHAT I *THOUGHT*, MORTY.
OKAY, JERRYS--

OH BOY!
THIS WAS A GOOD ARTICLE!
I LIKE TO READ THE MEDICATION ADVERTISEMENTS!
ASPIRING HOBBYIST MAGAZINE

--IT'S TIME TO DUEL!

UM. BETH?
WHAT, JERRY?

DO WE *HAVE* TO FIGHT?
FOR THE LAST TIME, JERRY, *YES*.

I DON'T KNOW WHY YOU GUYS ARE SO AGAINST IT.
IT'S NOT LIKE YOU GUYS CAN FEEL *PAIN*, ANYWAY.

YEAH, YOU KEEP *SAYING* THAT...
I'M NOT SURE WHERE YOU GOT THAT IDEA, WE DEFINITELY *DO*--

TWEEEEET

SWIMMING JERRY! WIZARD JERRY! I CHOOSE YOU!
FIGHT!

WHAP
OWWW!
EHH! EHH! TAKE THAT!
NO! NO. DON'T DO IT! NO!
ZAP
ZAP
AAAAND THAT!
DOOF
NOO!
THE LAST WIZARD WHO HURT ME WAS AT MY TENTH BIRTHDAY PARTY!
AND HE WASN'T EVEN A REAL WIZARD!
JESUS, THIS IS A MESS.

ARE ALL JERRY FIGHTS LIKE THIS?
WE'RE INDIE, MORTY. VERY, *VERY* INDIE.

LIKE IN THE SENSE THAT "INDIE" IS OFTEN JUST A EUPHEMISM FOR "COMPLETELY UNREVISED"?
TWEEE

WHATEVER, JERRYS. COME ON, LET'S ALL GO TAKE A NAP IN THE BIG TENT.

Y-Y-YOU MEAN IT, BETH? WE CAN SLEEP IN THE TENT WITH YOU?
SURE, FINE.
I'VE GOT THIS HEATER I RUN IN THERE THAT SAYS "DO NOT USE IN TENT, DANGEROUS FUMES," SO THERE'S A FIFTY-FIFTY SHOT WE WON'T EVEN WAKE UP.

BEEEETH!

BEEETH!
BEEEETH!

BEEEETH!
WHAT, WRESTLER JERRY?! I'M RIGHT HERE, WHAT?

YOU SA--WHOO RUNNING REALLY TAKES IT OUT OF YOU.
YOU SAID. YOU MISSED. SCRAPBOOKING. SO--
--SO. I BROUGHT YOU PAPER.

NO, JERRY. I SAID I MISSED MAKING VALUABLE MEMORIES. SCRAPBOOKING WOULD IMPLY I HAVE ANYTHING WORTH SCRAPBOOKING ABOUT.

OH... HEL-LO...
UHHH...

LOST:
EVIL MORTY
ANSWERS TO "MORTY," DUH, WHY WOULD YOU EVEN ASK THAT
REWARD FOR RETURN $$$$$$$$$$$$$$$$$$$$$
REWARD, EH?

MORTY, YOU'RE SUPPOSED TO TELL YOUR MOTHER IF YOU'RE A FUGITIVE WITH A CASH REWARD. I TAUGHT YOU BETTER THAN THAT.
N-N-NO YOU DIDN'T! AND THAT'S NOT ME! I'M NOT A MORTY!

NO?
N-N-NO! I'M... UH...

A MORTY-TYPE JERRY!

HUH?
HUH?
HUH?
HUH?

JERRY
YEAH! UH, I'M A JERRY, LIKE YOU GUYS! THAT'S WHY I'M HERE!

WELL, HOLD ON. THEN HOW COME YOU LOOK LIKE A MORTY?
SAME REASON YOU LOOK LIKE A WIZARD.

OHHHHH.
HE'S GOT A POINT.
HOLD ON.

I DON'T BUY IT.
WE DO!
UHHH...

BIG SURPRISE.
SERIOUSLY, THOUGH.

WE BELIEVE HIM.
NO ONE WOULD LIE ABOUT BEING ONE OF US IF THEY WEREN'T ONE OF US, BETH.

YEAH. IN THIS REALITY, WE'RE ACTUALLY CLASSIFIED AS A FUNGUS.

OKAY, OKAY, FINE. MORTY. IF YOU'RE A JERRY...

...THEN FIGHT ANOTHER JERRY.
HUNGRY FOR APPLES
GULP!

IF THIS IS YOUR FIRST NIGHT, YOU *HAVE* TO FIGHT!
WOO! YEAH! THAT'S FROM A MOVIE!

EW.
AW, GEEZ... OKAY...

WHOO.
OKAY.
FIGHTIN' YOUR INTERDIMENSIONAL DAD.

MORE LIKE YOUR *BUFF* INTERDIMENSIONAL DAD!
WOOOO!
GET 'IM!
HUNGRY FOR APPLES

I'LL BET YOU SKIPPED LEG DAY.

HUH?

AAUUUUUGH!
WHOOA!

GNAWGA CHOMP

GRRR...
SKIIIIID

RAAAAAGH!
FLEXXX

HNNGH!

PBBBBBTTT!

PEW

RICK!
OH, DAD.
HEY THERE, RICK.

WUBBA LUBBA @#$%ING DUB DUB, BETH.
NEXT: TAMA-GOTCHA!

Rick and Morty

Pocket Like You Stole It

VS

CHAPTER FOUR

RICK AND MORTY & THE POCKET MORTYS IN:

POCKET LIKE YOU STOLE IT!

PART FOUR: TAMA-GOTCHYA!

SCRIPT: TINI HOWARD
ART: MARC ELLERBY
COLORS: KATY FARINA
LETTERS: CRANK!

GO, JERRYS! ALL OF YOU! FIGHT!
FIGHT FOR YOUR SON!
WHAT?

YOUR... SON?
YOUR SON, MORTY.
THIS GUY? NO, MY DARLING BETH, THIS IS A MORTY JERRY.

NO, IT ISN'T, YOU IDIOTS! IT'S OBVIOUSLY JUST MORTY!
BETH? WERE YOU... DISHONEST WITH US?

BETH, DR. DONGLE SAID WE HAVE TO BE HONEST WITH ONE ANOTHER.
OH, HE'S NOT EVEN A DOCTOR, HE'S A LICENSED THERAPIST...

OH MY GOD, JUST GO! HE'S GETTING AWAY!

TRUST ME, MORTY, YOU'RE GONNA BE A LOT HAPPIER THIS WAY.
LEMME GO, RICK!

I CAN'T DO THAT, MORTY.
YOU CAN MUH--URRRRRP--AKE UP A NOBLE REASON IF YOU LIKE, BUT REALLY, I JUST WANNA MAKE YOU FIGHT STUFF.
Y-Y-YOU'RE GONNA PAY FOR THIS!

NOT LIKELY, MORTY, I ONLY PAY FOR LEGAL ADVICE TO GET OUT OF PAYING FOR THI--

WHACK
HURK!

URR! UR! UR! URRR!!
BEEEETHHH!!

LEMME--LEMME GO! I DON'T WANNA FIGHT ANYONE, I JUST WANNA SAVE THE MORTYS, S-SO I CAN GO HOME AND EAT FROZEN PIZZA AND LOOK AT THE WEIRD PARTS OF THE INTERNET!

OH, JERRY. ALL YOU JERRYS. YOU *IDIOTS*.
ALL I'VE NEEDED IS A *REASON*.

AND YOU JUST *GAVE ME ONE*.

CRKKZZZZZZT

JESUS, DAD! IF YOU TAZE THEM ALL, I'M GONNA HAVE TO BOTTLE FEED THEM AGAIN, AND THEY ALWAYS GET NIPPLE CONFUSION!
BETH. YOU KNOW I DON'T EVER WANT TO HEAR YOU SAY "NIPPLE."

COME OUT, COME OUT, WHEREVER YOU ARE...

PBBRRRRRTTT
UGH, SMELLS LIKE FEAR AND--

--KOMBUCHA.

HEH, IT'S GOOD FOR YOUR GUT--

CRK KZZZZT

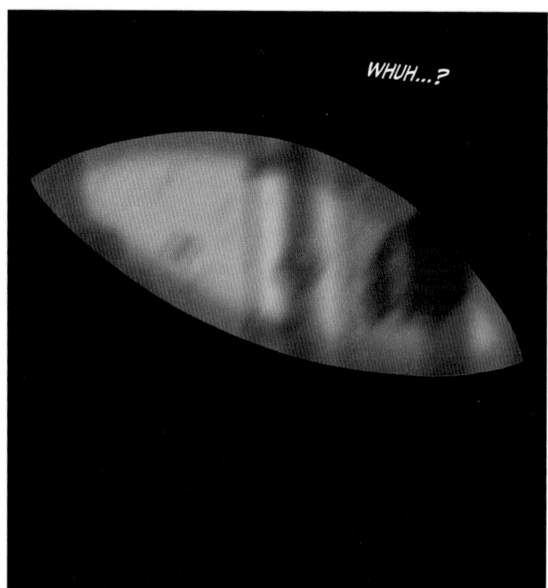
WHUH...?

AW, GEEZ. NOT AGAIN.
OKAY, MORTY. THINK.

WHERE AM I? WHERE ARE ALL THESE FLIES COMING FROM?

N-NO! AUGH, GOD, RIIIICK!

BEEEP
BEEEP
BEEEEP

SHHH. YOU'RE IN TIME OUT, MORTY.
BEEEP BEEEP BEEEEP

BEEEP BEEEP BEEEEP

I KNOW, LITTLE GUY. YOU FILLED THAT SCREEN UP WITH YOUR PIXEL-DOOKIE PRETTY FAST! I'M IMPRESSED.
BUT YOU'VE SHOWN THAT YOU'RE NOT RESPONSIBLE WITH, YANNO. FREEDOM.
BEEEEP BEEEP BEEEP BEEEEP

I KNOW, YOU WANT YOUR DOODIES CLEANED UP, BUT THEN I'D HAVE TO PUSH A **BUTTON**, AND NOW I'M OVER **HERE**...
I'M NOT GOOD WITH PETS, MO--**URRRP**--ORTY, THAT SHOULD BE OBVIOUS.
BEEP BEEP BEEP **BE--**

EEP-- OH! OH, I CAN STOP BEEPING, HEH.
I KNOW ABOUT THE POCKET RICKS!

YOU... **WHAT?**

Y-YEAH! HIPPIE RICK TOLD ME ABOUT IT! AND HOW MUCH IT SUCKED, AND--
I CAN HELP! I CAN FREE BOTH RICKS AND MORTYS FROM THE COUNCIL!
BULLSH**T.

IT WAS TOTAL BULLS**T.
GRANDPA RICK?

SHOOOMP
MORTY? YOU EVER BEEN THE BEST AT ANYTHING?
NO?
RIGHT, OF COURSE NOT.

"BE THE VERY BEST," THEY'D ALWAYS SAY. AND WHAT KINDA UNREACHABLE GOAL IS THAT, ANYWAY?
IT'S CRAP, MORTY. IT'S JUST CRAP.

THEY'D PUSH US, MAKE US FIGHT, WORK US ALL DAY.
ALL TO BE THE BEST.
AND WE ALWAYS THOUGHT...

...Y'KNOW, IF SOMEONE ELSE WANTS YOU TO BE THE BEST...

...YOU CAN JUST TAKE 'EM OUT AS A WAY OF CROSSING 'EM OFF THE LIST.

IT'S NOT ANY BETTER NOW, THOUGH, RIGHT? THE COUNCIL OF RICKS MAKES YOU DO WHAT THEY SAY, SO YOU'RE STILL STUCK FOLLOWING SOMEONE'S STUPID RULES!
YE--URRRP--AH, MORTY, BUT LIKE, IT'S A SOCIAL CONTRACT.
I GIVE UP MY COMPLETE FREEDOM AND THEY...
UH...

HEY, NOW THAT YOU MENTION IT, THEY DON'T REALLY DO CRAP FOR ME, MORTY. YOU MIGHT HAVE A POINT.
MUCH AS I HATE SAYING THAT.

RIGHT! SO LET'S TAKE 'EM OUT, LIKE YOU DID THE OTHER GYMS! I'LL HELP YOU GET RID OF THE COUNCIL OF RICKS, AND-AND-AND YOU CAN HELP ME FREE ALL THE POCKET MORTYS!
MORTY.

EVEN IF WE DO THAT, YOUR LITTLE MORTY FRIENDS ARE PROBABLY A MESS. YOU CAN'T UNCHIP A MORTY, IT TURNS THEIR BRAINS TO BANANA PUDDING.
LIKE, MORE THAN USUAL. WE'RE TALKING JERRY-LEVELS OF PUDDING BRAIN.

I DON'T...
I DON'T THINK THAT'S TRUE, RICK...

I MEAN, I'M PRETTY SURE WE'D BE OKAY, IF OUR CHIP, LIKE... FELL OUT, FOR EXAMPLE?

WHAT MAKES YOU SAY *THAT*, MORTY?
OH, *HEH*. YOU KNOW, *UHM*. JUST A HYP-HYPOTHESIS.

UH-HUH. DON'T HURT YOURSELF ON THAT WORD, MORTY.
BUT YOU HAVE A POINT ABOUT THE COUNCIL OF RICKS.

THE COUNCIL IS FORMED OF THE MOST STABLE, BORING RICKS. THE NOBLE RICKS.
BUNCHA KILLJOYS.

WHICH MEANS THEY ACTUALLY MIGHT BE ABLE TO BE CONVINCED THROUGH A LONG, BORING ARGUMENT. OR AT LEAST DISTRACTED.

WHUH--
ZWIRT
RIGHT AFTER WE FIGHT OUR WAY THROUGH THE MUTATED MORTY GUARDS!
WUBBA LUBBA DUB DUUUUUB!

THE CITADEL OF RICKS.

WH-WHY, RICK? WHY DIDN'T YOU TELL ME ABOUT THE MUTATED MORTY GUARDS *BEFORE* YOU SHOT THE PORTAL GUN?
GEE, YOU'RE RIGHT, MORTY. I'M USUALLY SO CONSIDERATE REGARDING THE ANXIETIES OF OTHERS.
WHUMP
ANYWAY, WE PROBABLY WANNA TABLE THIS DISCUSSION FOR NOW.

BROOOOOOOO!
AUUUUGHHH!
EET MEATS 4 GAINZ

OHGODOHMYGODRICKRICKRICK IT'S A MUTANT MORTY I CAN'T FIGHT THAT LOOK AT HIS LEGS I DIDN'T KNOW THIGHS HAD THOSE MUSCLES--
HOLD STILL, THAT'S NOT A MUTANT MORTY--

IT'S JUST A RARE CROSSFIT MORTY!
MORTY, GO! FIGHT IT! KNOCK IT OUT, I NEED THAT ONE, THEY'RE SUPER RARE!

LIIIIIIIIFTS!

MAAACROOOOOS...
Y-Y-YOU DON'T WANNA DO THAT, PAL--

I'M CHOCK FULL O' CARBS.

NOOOOOOOO!!
RICK, NOW!

EAT MY BALLS.

THIS GUY'S GONNA LOVE THE MORTY DAY CARE. CRAPPY FOOD AND TONS OF HARD LABOR.
GONNA GET HIM RI-- URRRRRP-- IPPED.
GEE-- *GASP*--HEE-- *PANT*--EEZ RICK, I--I REALLY GOT HIM GOOD THERE.

HUH? YEAH, SURE, LET'S HOPE ALL THE MUTANT MORTYS HAVE A GLUTEN INTOLERANCE.
MOVE IT, MORTY.

OKAY, UH, LET'S DO THIS.

BRING IT, MUTANT MOR--
OH GOD.

AW, GEEZ.
C'MON, MORTY, I CHOOSE YOU! KICK SOME ASS!
EHHH... I DON'T KNOW, RICK. I DON'T KNOW IF I NEED TO NECESSARILY FIGHT THEM...
HEYYY THERE, BUDDY.

YEEAAAHHH, GET 'IM!
GUH!
WHAP WHAP WHAP WHAP

MORTY VS. PANTS ON HEAD MUTANT MORTY
CRY
KICK
KOMBUCHA FART
RUN

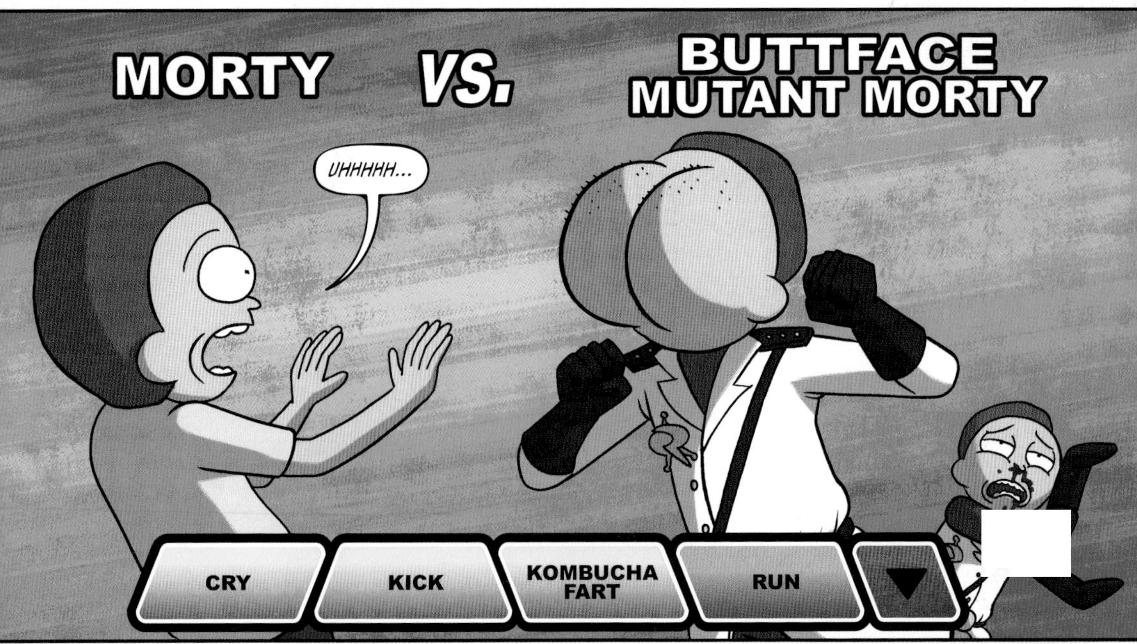
MORTY VS. BUTTFACE MUTANT MORTY
UHHHHH...
CRY
KICK
KOMBUCHA FART
RUN

LEMME GO LEMME GO LEMME GO--

D-D-DON'T MAKE ME *HURT* YOU!
SPANK SPANK SPANK SPANK

MORTY VS. ARM HEAD MUTANT MORTY
CRY
THROW
KOMBUCHA FART
RUN

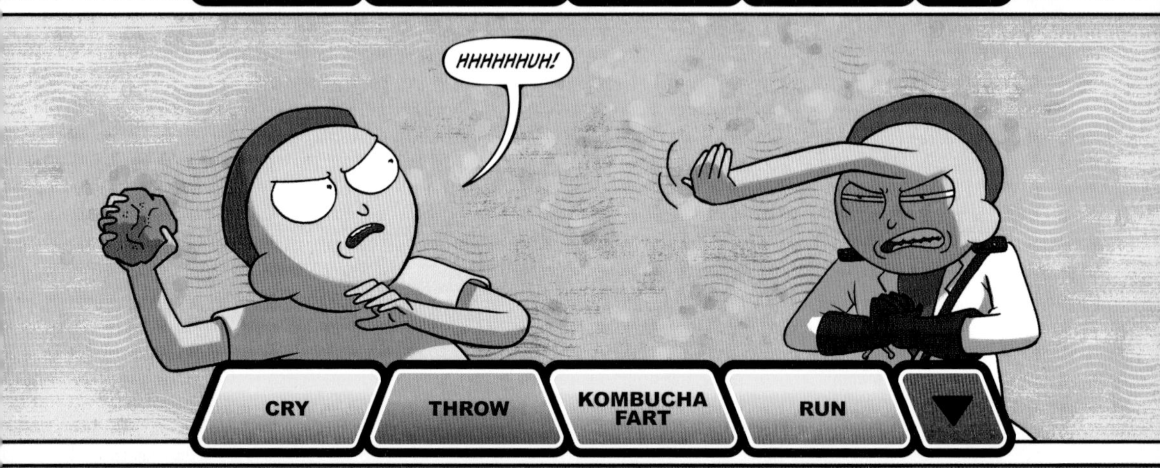
HHHHHHUH!
CRY
THROW
KOMBUCHA FART
RUN

RIIIICK, RICK, HE CAUGHT THE ROCK I'M OUTTA IDEAS.
HM? OH.
CRNKL

JUUUUST A SEC.

FZZZAP

RICK! WHY DIDN'T YOU JUST DO THAT IN THE FIRST PLACE?
OH, I'M SORRY, MORTY, IS THAT HOW GAMES ARE PLAYED?
WHUMP

JUST JUMP ON AHEAD, NO STRUGGLE, NO FUN?
YOU REMEMBER THE GAMESHARK, MORTY? COURSE YOU DON'T.
IT'S UNETHICAL, MORTY.

THIS IS ABOUT ETHICS IN MORTY BATTLING, MORTY.
IS IT, RICK?
IS IT?

SHH. INSIDE THERE SITS THE COUNCIL OF RICKS. YOU GOTTA USE YOUR BRAINS, MORTY.
YOU GOTTA-- URRRP--GOTTA TALK TO 'EM, OKAY?
UHHH...
THEY'RE GONNA BE TERRIBLE, BUT YOU'RE LIKE, AN ADVOCATE, OR WHATEVER.

I FEEL LIKE YOU'RE THROWING ME TO THE WOLVES, HERE, RICK.
DON'T BE RIDICULOUS, MORTY, IT'S JUST LIKE TALKING TO YOUR OL' GRANDAD...

...ZERO RISK AWARENESS, CRIPPLING INSECURITY, AND GODLIKE POWERS.
NEXT: F**K-SAVE!

CHAPTER FIVE

I'M READY, RICK.

I FIGURED IT OUT.
I'LL GO IN AND TALK TO THEM, BUT TO FREE MYSELF AND THE OTHER MORTYS, I'LL NEED A PORTAL GUN, A MICROVERSAL BATTERY...

...ONE OF THOSE RED CRYSTALS FROM YOUR SUICIDE MACHINE, THE LOST VHS BOX SET OF **FULL HOUSE** WITH THE EPISODE WHERE KIMMY GIBLER GETS SHINGLES...

...A-A-AND GWENDOLYN. IF I'M GONNA GO IN THERE AND PROBABLY DIE, I WANNA SEE HER ONE LAST TIME.
MORTY--

FOR ONCE, I'M NOT LY--URRRP--ING TO YOU.
YOU'RE GONNA GO IN THERE AND TALK TO 'EM.
OH.

C-C-CAN I SEE GWENDOLYN ANYWAY?
AND HAVE, LIKE, WEAPONS?

IF YOU GO IN THERE STRAPPED, IT'S JUST GOING TO SHOW THEM YOU'RE READY TO FIGHT.
THAT YOU'RE JUST A DUMB OL' BATTLING PET.
IF IT'S RICK-LEVEL FREEDOM YOU SEEK...

...YOU GOTTA DISPLAY RICK-LEVEL INTELLECT.
RICK AND MORTY
& THE POCKET MORTYS IN
POCKET LIKE YOU STOLE IT!
PART FIVE: F**K-SAVE
SCRIPT: TINI HOWARD
ART: MARC ELLERBY
COLORS: KATY FARINA
LETTERS: CRANK!

OOH! OOH OOH, I THINK MY CAT MORTY IS HAVING KITTENS! THIS ONE'S GONNA BE NAMED PICHAEL...
BEEP BEEP BEEP

GET IT, MO--URRRRRP--ORTY? IT'S A REFERENCE TO AN EARLIER NAME WE ENCOUNTERED?
I'M GOING IN, RICK.

I'VE GOT A RACE OF TINY POCKET MES TO SAVE.

I'M HERE TO SEE THE COUNCIL.
REALLY? I FEEL LIKE I'M HERE TO MAKE A DIFFERENCE.
ME, I JUST LOVE KILLING.

LET ME IN.
UH, DO YOU HAVE A PASSKEY?

N-NO, I JUST, UH--
IF YOU DON'T, A SCATTERBEAM WILL OPEN THE LOCKS RIGHT UP.
MOST OF THE RICKS WHO AREN'T SUPPOSED TO BE HERE JUST BREAK IN WITH ONE OF THOSE.
Z
PAT PAT
PAT PAT

BWOOP BWOOP
BEEPBEEPBEEP
SWISH

HEH--OH YEAH. I'VE GOT ONE OF THOSE, SURE, OF COURSE.
I JUST FIGURED YOU'D, UH, TRY AND STOP ME IF I WHIPPED IT OUT?

I MEAN, WE'RE MOSTLY HERE FOR KILLIN'.
AND THAT'S NOT REALLY A KILLABLE OFFENSE...

EXCUSE ME JUST, JUST ONE SECOND, GUYS.

RICK, I NEED YOUR UH, SKITTER... BALL...
SCATTERBEAM. AND NO.
CAN YOU PUT THAT STUPID THING DOWN?! THOSE GAMES ARE FOR BABIES, ANYWAY!
MORTY, THERE IS NO SURER WAY TO MAKE YOURSELF SOUND LIKE A GIANT BABY THAN TO DECREE THAT ANYTHING IS, QUOTE, "FOR BABIES."
ANYWAY, I MADE MYSELF PRETTY CLEAR WHAT IT WAS GOING TO TAKE TO GET THROUGH THIS CHALLENGE.
RICK LEVEL INTELLECT...
WUBBA LUBBA DUB DUBBBBB!
OOOF!
WHAP
GUM

RICK-LEVEL INTELLECT, HEH.
WHAT WOULD RICK DO, HEH.
RICK LIKE NO ONE IS WATCHING.

WVRRR
STAFF ONLY!!

YOU WANT SOME RICK-LEVEL INTELLECT?
A FIRE EXIT?

GET READY FOR A DEEP-RICKING.
A FIRE EXIT?

AW, GEEZ.

LIKE WHAT YOU SEE?

QUITE A COLL-- **URRRP**--ECTION WE'VE ESTABLISHED.

THESE ARE ALL OF THE KNOWN MORTYS.
SOME ARE CLONES, SOME ARE THE REAL THING, SOME...

...WERE NOT SO LUCKY.

YEAH, UM, YOU SAY "LUCKY" LIKE THE BETTER OPTION IS BEING TRAPPED ON A WALL IN THIS PLACE.
OH, YOU HAVE THINGS TO SAY, IT SEEMS. PERFECT.
CLK

WHRRRRRR

I CAME HERE TO FIGHT MORTYS AND CHEW BUBBLE GUM
SHOW ME WHAT YOU GOT

YIPPIE KI YAY
WHAT IS THIS?

IT'S MUSCLEBOT!
MUSCLEBOT? YOU'RE NOT GOING TO TEMPT ME TO FIGHT ANYTHING, RICK.

IT'S RIQ. RIQ V. AND THIS IS MUSCLEBOT. HE'S NOT GONNA FIGHT YOU, DESPITE WHAT HE THINKS.

YOU FEEL LUCKY PUNK DO YA
HE'S HERE SO YOU CAN GET ALL YOUR BULLCRAP ACTION STAR DIALOGUE OUT OF YOUR SYSTEM--

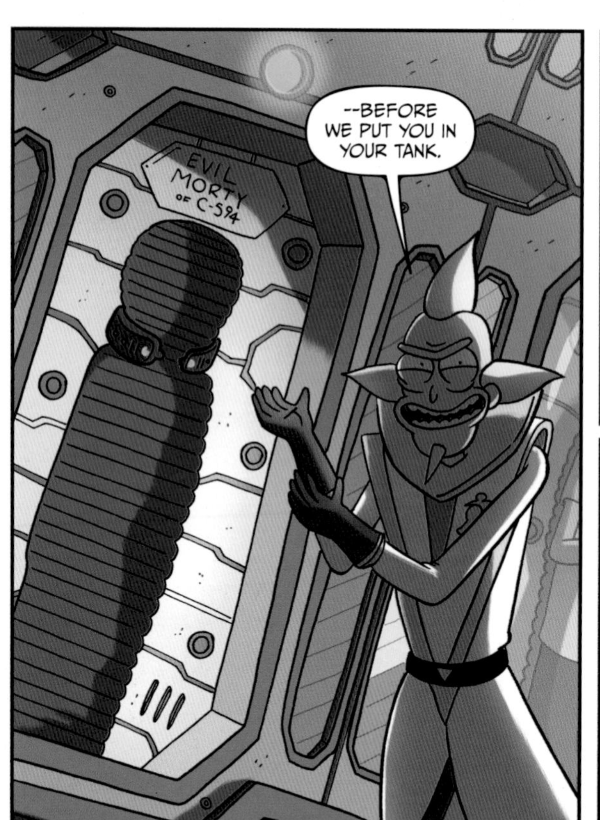
EVIL MORTY OF C-594
--BEFORE WE PUT YOU IN YOUR TANK.

I'M NOT EVIL M--
GET TO THE CHOPPER

Y-Y-Y'KNOW WHAT? SURE. I'LL BE *WHATEVER YOU THINK I AM.*

HASTA LA VISTA
KZZZT
I WILL SLAP EVERYONE IN THIS ROOM IF I HAVE TO
THAT ONE WAS FROM BRIDEZILLAS, NOT AN ACTION MOVIE
BUT I LIKE IT

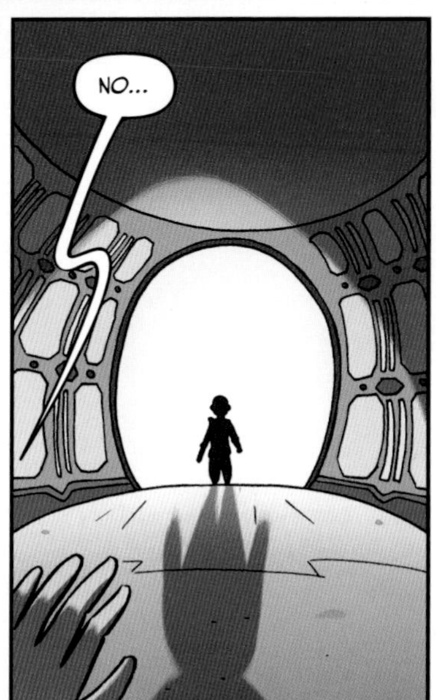
NO...

IT CAN'T BE...

GWENDOLYN!

UNNHHHHH...
KZZZT

WHOOOOSH

OOF!
GUH... WEN...

GROSS. IT'S A QUANTUM TAZER, MORTY.
IT'S JUST A GIANT TAZER THAT CAN TAKE ANY FORM YOU FIND APPEALING.
YOU'RE SO GROSS.

MORTY. SIT THE HELL DOWN.
NO! I'M *TIRED* OF THIS! I HAVE BEEN TRYING TO GO HOME AND EAT A PIZZA ON THE TOILET WITH THE DOOR LOCKED FOR WHAT FEELS LIKE ***MY ENTIRE LIFE!***

THEN GO.
YEAH, MORTY, JUST GO.
FIRE EXIT

WHAT'S THE CATCH?
WHAT?
IT'S NOT *OUR* CATCH, PAL.

YOU MORTYS ARE CHIPPED TO KEEP YOU DOCILE, IT'S TRUE.
AND YES, WITHOUT IT YOU'D ALL RISE UP AND TRY TO TAKE OVER. LIKE WE DID.

SO GIVE US THAT CHANCE!
EVEN IF WE FAIL, Y'KNOW, WE'RE SUPPOSED TO BE HAPPY ABOUT TRYING... *UH...* FROM THE AFTERLIFE, OR WHATEVER.
DEAD. DEAD BUT HAPPY? OR SOMETHING?

UH-HUH.

AND... UH...

KID, YOU'RE WASTING OUR TIME.
IF YOU'RE NOT READY FOR THE TANK, WE HAVE A RARE STICKY POPSICLE HANDS MORTY THAT EVERYONE ELSE REFUSES TO TOUCH, YOU COULD FIGHT HIM?

N-NO, I, *UH*... I HAVE AN IDEA--

I KNOW THAT LOOK, HE'S STALLING.
GUARDS!

N-NO, I, UH, I'VE GOT AN IDEA! ABOUT-- HEY!

GET OFF ME-- UH, NO, IT'S ABOUT, UHMMM...

C'MON... RICK LEVEL INTELLECT RICK LEVEL INTELLECT...

YOU DON'T WANNA TRAP ME HERE.

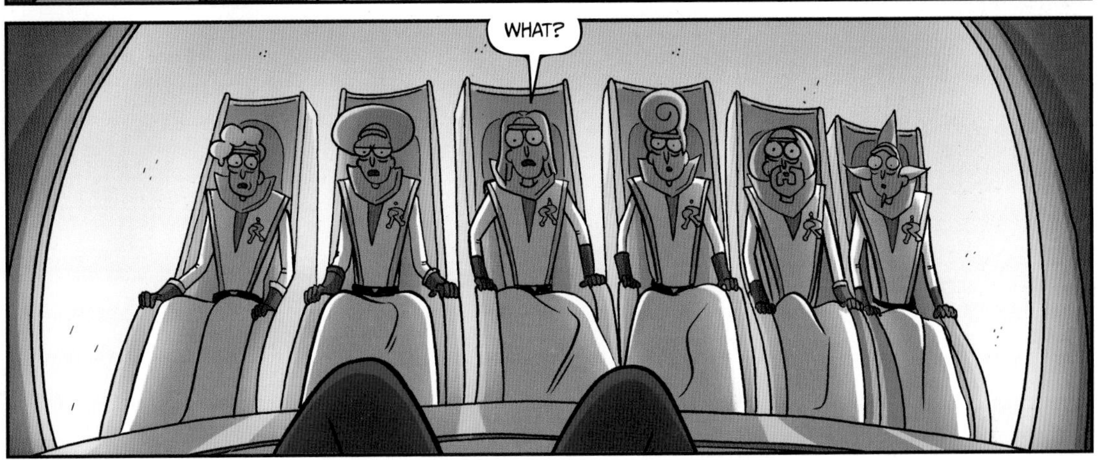
WHAT?

YOU KNOW AS WELL AS I DO THAT MY RICK IS A **SPECIAL** KIND OF TWISTED.
AND HE'S JUST LOOKING FOR A REASON TO GO, *UH*, FUTURE... SPACE... MEDIEVAL ON YOUR ASSES.

AND I'M SURE I'M NOT THE ONLY ONE. LET ME FREE--AND THE OTHER MORTYS, TOO.
OR ACCEPT THAT THE **SAME** REVOLUTION THAT GOT YOU **YOUR** JOBS IS ABOUT TO PUT YOU **OUT** OF A JOB.

DID HE GET A CHANCE TO TALK TO MUSCLEBOT? BECAUSE HE SHOULD HAVE GOTTEN THAT OUT OF HIS SYSTEM.
NICE TRY, KID. THAT'S WHAT THE MANIPULATION CHIPS ARE FOR.
EVEN IF WE TAKE 'EM OFF NOW, YOU MORTYS WOULD HAVE THE BRAINS OF BABY FOOD.

YOU'RE **WRONG** ABOUT THAT.

HAHAHAHA
I'M-I'M GONNA PEE, GUYS YOU HAVE TO STOP-- I'M... I'M SERIOUSLY GONNA PEE MY PANTS.

YOU **ARE** WRONG. ***I'VE*** BEEN CHIPPED AND UNCHIPPED.
SEVERAL TIMES.

NO YOU HAVEN'T.

YES-HUH. THE ONE ON MY NECK HAS BEEN ON AND OFF SO MANY TIMES IT DOESN'T--

WHUH!
H-H-HEY!

BOOM. BUTTCHEEK CHIP.
STANDARD FOR MORTYS WHO COULDN'T FIND THEIR OWN ASS WITH A MAP AND A RICK TO GUIDE THEM.

LIKE YOU SAID, YOUR RICK IS A SPECIAL KIND OF TWISTED.
HE'S BEEN CONTROLLING YOU IN SECRET ALL ALONG.

MAN, AS A RULE WE'RE FAIRLY DEVIOUS, BUT MOST OF US ARE AT LEAST *SOMEWHAT* HONEST WITH OUR MORTYS.
THAT ONE FROM YOUR REALITY IS A *MESS*.
YOUR WHOLE REALITY IS *WHACK*.
IS IT TRUE YOUR BOWIE DIED?!

THIS... THIS IS IMPOSSIBLE! I'VE BEEN CONTROLLED BY RICK THIS *WHOLE TIME?*

OHHHH MAN, RICK. YOU'VE BEEN WATCHING?
IS IT REALLY YOU, CONTROLLING ME? DO I JUST DO WHAT YOU COMMAND ME TO?
WANTING TO SAVE MORTYS, WAS THAT *YOUR* FAKE PLAN TO DISTRACT ME?

I *SEE*. I MUST *DO AS YOU COMMAND*.

FREEDOM FOR MORTYS! AAAIIIIYIYIYIYIYAAA!
GASP!

HEH-
HEH.
IT'S
GOOD TO
LAUGH.

AAAAAAAAUUUUUUGH!
OOHHHH MERCIFUL CRAP.
OH GOD HE'S EATING HIM.
HE'S EATING QUANTUM
RICK!
SPLAT
NYUP NYUP
STOP
HIM!
STOP THE
MORTY!

N-NO! NO PLEASE,
WE'LL SET THEM FREE,
JUST GIVE HIM HIS
ARM BACK!
NO
DON'T--
DON'T!

PLEASE, I CAN'T
RELEASE THE MORTYS
WITHOUT MY ARMS.
PLEE-HEE-HEESE
HAVE MERCY--
AAACK!
HRM.
OKAY,
MORTY.

FINISH
URRR--UP IN THERE,
LET'S BLOW THIS
PLACE.

GRRR... HEEEE... RRROOWWW...
KNOCK IT OFF, MORTY, WE'RE DONE HERE.

HUH? I'M JUST--YANNO. COMMANDED TO DESTROY, RICK.
B-B-BY YOU, RICK.

NO, YOU'RE NOT. YOU DID THAT ALL YOUR OWN.
JESUS, MORTY, HOW IS ANY KID SO PREDICTABLE? YOU KNOW, IF YOU WERE A LAB HAMSTER YOU'D BE DEAD BY NOW.
HUH?
WHAH?

THAT CHIP ISN'T A MANIPULATION CHIP, MORTY, IT'S PART OF AN OLD, OBSOLETE MP3 PLAYER I GLUED TO YOUR BUTT. REMEMBER ZUNE, MORTY? I HAD A ZUNE.
I'M NOT PROUD OF IT, BUT OF OUR TWO EMBARRASSMENTS TODAY, I'M NOT THE ONE WHO WAS TRICKED THREE TIMES OVER INTO TEARING APART A ROOM FULL OF MY GRANDFATHER'S ALTERNATE SELVES.
OHH...

C'MON, LET'S GET OUT OF HERE.

Y'KNOW, RICK...?

IT-IT-IT JUST MEANS THAT I ALWAYS HAD THAT FIGHT IN ME, RIGHT, RICK?
LIKE I GOT THAT BLOODLUST IN ME ALL ALONG!

I-I-I'M A *FIGHTER*, RICK! YOU KNOW?
I'VE GOT REAL MOXIE IN THE RING!
YOU KNOW WHAT, MORTY, THAT'S NOT A BAD POINT.

BRING IT IN, KID, YOU'RE A FIGHTER.

ZZZZZT

LATER.
FRIDAY NIGHT MORTY FIGHTS
WOOOOOO!
GRRRAH!
WUBBA LUBBA DUB DUB!
SKEPT
END.

POCKET MORTY TRADING CARDS!

Hey kids! Want to play **POCKET MORTYS**, but don't have a phone? Or-or-or maybe you do, but Mom spent the phone money on boxes of chardonnay again and Dad's been out of work for a while? You can play the old-fashioned way with these **POCKET MORTY CARDS!** Get an adult to help you cut them out!

URP Geez, Morty, get an *adult*? To help with *scissors*? No wonder the economy's in the toilet, kids can't even use a pair of *scissors* without a *lawsuit*.

Aw, geez, Rick. Just play **ROCK, PAPER, SCISSORS** for each Morty battle, okay, kids?

MER-MORTY 145 HP 

ROCK

FLOP 68

If your opponent beats Mer-Morty, you can splash them with water to revive your precious fishboy. Go on, it's fine. A game told you it was okay.

"....blub....blub...I crave the sweet release of death."

WEAKNESS

EVIL MORTY 666 HP 

SCISSORS

UNENDING DARKNESS 666

Evil Morty can only be defeated by a young priest and an old priest, working together in tandem. Make church fun with Pocket Mortys!

"And if thou gaze long into an abyss, the abyss will also gaze into thee." —Nietzsche

WEAKNESS

SPORK MORTY 50 HP   

ANY

ADAPTATION 45

Pudding? Sure! A salad? Maybe! Soup? Kind of! You can definitely eat almost anything with mild difficulty, if you've got a spork.

"The tines are basically useless for eating, but great for jabbing yourself in the gums."

   **WEAKNESS**

ROBOT MORTY 500 HP 

ROCK

CRUSH 250

Robot Morty's hands are useless for loving, and he can only crush. As such, he destroys any Morty he touches, friend or foe.

"I want to understand your human notions of love, but I'm just too strong."

 **WEAKNESS**

POP STAR MORTY 30 HP 

SCISSORS

PR 55

Pop Star Morty has a great PR team, and can dodge almost any attack!

"Oops, I swear I thought I was wearing underwear when I got out of that car."

 **WEAKNESS**

TUBBY MORTY 45 HP

HAM

STICKS AND STONES! 15

Tubby Morty is so happily full of pizza, he cannot be harmed by Rock-based attacks.

"Dip the crust in ranch dressing. Don't look at me like that, it's *amazing.*"

WEAKNESS

CRAZY CAT RICK 100 HP 

TRAINER

 **FORGET-ME-NOT** 

Crazy Cat Rick sometimes takes in so many Mortys that he forgets about a few, and they end up smushed under a stack of old magazines.

 **WEAKNESS**

HIPPIE MORTY 150 HP 

SPIRIT

 **WHATEVER, MAAAAN** 

Hippie Rick assumes your attacks are due to your own misaligned internal flora, and thusly is not affected. He also will not attack.

"God, this kombucha crap really does taste terrible."

 **WEAKNESS**

FERAL POCKET RICK 25 HP

ROCK

REVOLUTION 40

Feral Pocket Rick can become a trainer, if he wins a battle.

"grrrrr.....rrrrrrrrr.......awoooooo!!!"

WEAKNESS

WIZARD JERRY 33 HP

DAD

VANISH 10

After targeting another card for an attack, Jerry can not be targeted.

"Watch me make the sense of intimacy in my marriage disappear!"

WEAKNESS

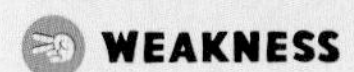

SWIMMING JERRY 23 HP

DAD

I JUST WANT TO BE LIKE YOU! 4

Jerry can do double damage to water-type characters.

"I ate a sandwich yesterday, is it safe to swim?"

WEAKNESS

WRESTLER JERRY 66 HP

DAD

SHAME-GRAPPLE 35

Wrestler Jerry can 'pin' another card for one turn, but the controlling player must weep softly into their hands for the duration.

"The mask gives me the freedom to show off my problem areas!"

WEAKNESS

COUPLES THERAPY JERRY 4 HP
WORM
NONE 1
Couples Therapy Jerry is completely useless unless Beth is present.
"*whimper*"
WEAKNESS

BUFF JERRY 45 HP
BUFF DAD
FLEX 13
Buff Jerry can flex, intimidating another player out of their turn.
"I'm not sure what 'macros' are, but I'm sure my trainer says to watch them!"
WEAKNESS

RIQ IV 250 HP
RICK
SPAY/NEUTER 100
Once per turn, Riq IV can render another card unusable by taking it from the player.
"Gimme that. You're having fun with that and I hate joy."
WEAKNESS

RICK PRIME 250 HP
RICK
GRAPPLE 100
Rick Prime cannot be affected by Morty type cards.
"It's a double-hopped IPA, meaning it's not for the faint of heart."
WEAKNESS

QUANTUM RICK 250 HP

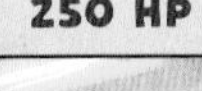

RICK

GLARE 100

Quantum Rick can do double damage if the opponent cannot answer a simple science question.

"Starbuck doesn't even make sense as a female character. It's like they're literally taking a st on my childhood."**

WEAKNESS

MAXIMUMS RICKIMUS 250 HP

RICK

TAKE ME SERIOUSLY 100

Maximums Rickimus does double damage on short-haired opponents.

"Fine, if you want these nobodies to grow up with Devo, I guess I'll pack my st and leave."**

WEAKNESS

ZETA ALPHA RICK 250 HP

RICK

HURTING YOU MAKES THE PAIN GO AWAY 100

Zeta Alpha Rick can attack twice per turn.

[Zeta Alpha Rick could not be reached for a quote, doesn't wanna talk about it.]

WEAKNESS

RICKTIMINUS SANCHEZIMINIUS 250 HP

RICK

SNEER 100

Ricktiminus Sancheziminius is not harmed by any opponent who has an Instagram.

"Why the hell would you ruin a classic by making it a musical, anyway?"

WEAKNESS

DAN HARMON is the Emmy® winning creator/executive producer of the comedy series *Community* as well as the co-creator/executive producer of Adult Swim™'s *Rick and Morty*™.

Harmon's pursuit of minimal work for maximum reward took him from stand-up to improv to sketch comedy, then finally to Los Angeles, where he began writing feature screenplays with fellow Milwaukeean Rob Schrab. As part of his deal with Robert Zemeckis at Imagemovers, Harmon co-wrote the feature film *Monster House*. Following this, Harmon co-wrote the Ben Stiller-directed pilot *Heat Vision and Jack*, starring Jack Black and Owen Wilson.

Disillusioned by the legitimate industry, Harmon began attending classes at nearby Glendale Community College. At the same time, Harmon and Schrab founded *Channel 101*, an untelevised non-profit audience-controlled network for undiscovered filmmakers, many of whom used it to launch mainstream careers, including the boys behind SNL's *Digital Shorts*. Harmon, along with Schrab, partnered with Sarah Silverman to create her Comedy Central series, *The Sarah Silverman Program*, where he served as head writer for the first season.

Harmon went on to create, write, and perform in the short-lived VH1 sketch series *Acceptable TV* before eventually creating the critically acclaimed and fan-favorite comedy *Community*. The show originally aired on NBC for five seasons before being acquired by Yahoo, which premiered season six of the show in March 2015. In 2009, he won an Emmy for Outstanding Music and Lyrics for the opening number of the 81st Annual Academy Awards.

Along with Justin Roiland, Harmon created the breakout Adult Swim™ animated series *Rick and Morty*™. The show premiered in December 2013 and quickly became a ratings hit. Harmon and Roiland have wrapped up season three, which premiered in 2017.

In 2014, Harmon was the star of the documentary *Harmontown*, which premiered at the SXSW Film Festival and chronicled his 20-city stand-up/podcast tour of the same name. The documentary was released theatrically in October 2014.

JUSTIN ROILAND grew up in Manteca, California, where he did the basic stuff children do. Later in life he traveled to Los Angeles. Once settled in, he created several popular online shorts for *Channel 101*.

Justin is afraid of his mortality and hopes the things he creates will make lots of people happy. Then maybe when modern civilization collapses into chaos, people will remember him and they'll help him survive the bloodshed and violence. Global economic collapse is looming. It's going to be horrible, and honestly, a swift death might be preferable than living in the hell that awaits mankind.

Justin also really hates writing about himself in the third person. I hate this. That's right. It's me. I've been writing this whole thing. Hi. The cat's out of the bag. It's just you and me now. There never was a third person. If you want to know anything about me, just ask. Sorry this wasn't more informative.

TINI HOWARD is a writer and swamp witch from the Carolina Wilds. Her work includes *Magdalena* from Image/Top Cow Comics, *Rick and Morty™: Pocket Like You Stole It* from Oni Press, and *Assassinistas* from IDW/Black Crown! Her previous work includes *Power Rangers: Pink* (BOOM! Studios), *The Skeptics* (Black Mask Studios), and a contribution to the hit *Secret Loves of Geek Girls*, from Dark Horse Comics. She lives with her husband, Blake, and her son, Orlando, who is a cat.

MARC ELLERBY is a comics illustrator living in Essex, UK. He has worked on such titles as *Doctor Who*, *Regular Show*, and *The Amazing World of Gumball*. His own comics (which you should totally check out!) are *Chloe Noonan: Monster Hunter* and *Ellerbisms*. You can read some comics if you like at marcellerby.com.

KATY FARINA is a freelance comic artist and illustrator from Charlotte. Her work includes *Amazing World of Gumball* OGN volumes 1 and 2, *Capture Creatures*, and *Steven Universe*. Outside of drawing comics, reading comics, and thinking about comics, she... uh, usually just goes to her local comic shop. She loves a good cup of coffee, and coffee loves her. Her greatest passion is to tell good stories that will inspire others!

CHRIS CRANK has worked on several recent Oni Press books like *The Sixth Gun*, *Heartthrob*, *Angel City*, and others. Maybe you've seen his letters in *Revival*, *Hack/Slash*, *God Hates Astronauts*, or *Dark Engine* from Image. Or perhaps you've read *Lady Killer* or *Sundowners* from Dark Horse. Heck, you might even be reading the award winning *Battlepug* at battlepug.com right now! Catch him on Twitter: @ccrank!